★ THE NEXT GOAT

C. J. STROUD

CORINA JEFFRIES

PowerKiDS press

Published in 2025 by The Rosen Publishing Group, Inc.
2544 Clinton Street, Buffalo, NY 14224

First Edition

Editor: Greg Roza
Book Design: Rachel Rising

Photo Credits: Cover, ZUMA Press, Inc./Alamy Stock Photo; Cover, pp. 1, 4, 6, 8, 10, 12, 14, 16, 18, 20, 22, 23, 24 Pixacon/Shutterstock.com; Cover Farhanz9/Shutterstock.com; Cover, p. 1 Alhovik/Shutterstock.com; p. 4 Mtsaride/Shutterstock.com; pp. 5, 9, 17, 21 ASSOCIATED PRESS/AP Images; pp. 7, 11, 15 Cal Sport Media/Alamy Stock Photo; p. 10 3d brained/Shutterstock.com; p. 12 https://commons.wikimedia.org/wiki/File:Buckeyes_logo.svg; p. 13 Grindstone Media Group/Shutterstock.com; p. 16 Bonya_06/Shutterstock.com; p. 18 jjaf/Shutterstock.com; p. 19 ZUMA Press, Inc./Alamy Stock Photo.

Library of Congress Cataloging-in-Publication Data

Names: Jeffries, Corina, author.
Title: C.J. Stroud / Corina Jeffries.
Description: Buffalo, NY : PowerKids Press, 2025. | Series: The next GOAT | Includes index.
Identifiers: LCCN 2024031102 (print) | LCCN 2024031103 (ebook) | ISBN 9781499449679 (library binding) | ISBN 9781499449662 (paperback) | ISBN 9781499449686 (ebook)
Subjects: LCSH: Stroud, C. J., 2001- | Quarterbacks (Football)–United States–Biography–Juvenile literature. | Football players–United States–Biography–Juvenile literature.
Classification: LCC GV939.S7493 J44 2025 (print) | LCC GV939.S7493 (ebook) | DDC 796.332092 [B]–dc23/eng/20240709
LC record available at https://lccn.loc.gov/2024031102
LC ebook record available at https://lccn.loc.gov/2024031103

Manufactured in the United States of America

CPSIA Compliance Information: Batch #CWPK25. For Further Information contact Rosen Publishing at 1-800-237-9932.

CONTENTS

MEET C. J.!

Coleridge Bernard "C. J." Stroud IV was born on October 3, 2001. He grew up in Rancho Cucamonga, California. It soon became clear to his family that he was a natural-born **athlete**.

Stroud has always done well in sports, and he mostly loves football. He started winning **championships** in youth football. Now that Stroud is a starting quarterback in the National Football League (NFL), he's ready to prove himself again. He plays for the Houston Texans.

In his rookie, or first, year with the Texans, Stroud led the team to the playoffs. He also earned the Associated Press (AP) **Offensive** Rookie of the Year award.

YOUTH SPORTS

Stroud was drawn to sports as a child. He played football and basketball at a young age and amazed the coaches in his youth leagues.

Stroud's football coach as a child, Willie Munford, said that when he was 9 years old, Stroud could throw the football 50 yards (45.7 m)! That's twice as far as most kids that age can throw. And he was very **accurate**. Munford was Stroud's youth coach for five years. During that time, Stroud led the team to two youth league championships!

WHAT THEY'RE SAYING

"In 30 years, I've never had a quarterback like that."

—Willie Munford

Stroud also loved playing basketball as a kid, but his true love became football.

STAYING HUMBLE

Growing up, life was difficult for Stroud and his family. His father received a long prison sentence in 2015, and his mother Kimberly worked hard to support Stroud and his older sister and two older brothers.

Stroud says his mother kept him **humble**. During a youth basketball championship, Stroud and his teammates started celebrating before the end of the game. Stroud's mom came to the bench and told him to behave himself! The moment made a lasting mark on Stroud.

WHAT THEY'RE SAYING

"My parents did a great job raising me as such to be a humble young man, to understand how quick you get [success] is how quick [that success] can be taken away."

—C. J. Stroud

Kimberly Stroud once said about her son: "I'm amazed at how **resilient** he is. C. J. is the most amazing human I have ever met."

HIGH SCHOOL YEARS

Stroud's father went to prison when Stroud was just 13. The problems for his family were great. He often played sports with worn-out gear. Without money for a private coach, Stroud taught himself all he could about football.

Stroud's hard work paid off. In his senior, or final, year with the Rancho Cucamonga High School Cougars, he passed for 3,878 yards (3,546 m) and 47 touchdowns! That year, the local newspaper, the *Daily Bulletin*, named Stroud offensive player of the year.

Stroud connects his belief in Christianity and love of football to his father, who was a pastor, or church leader.

THE OHIO BUCKEYES

After high school, Stroud chose to go to The Ohio State University to play for the OSU Buckeyes. The Buckeyes are a part of the Big Ten **Conference**, which is the oldest Division I conference. Division I is the highest level of college sports in the United States.

Although he played for only two seasons, Stroud set several important records for the Buckeyes. In his first full year, he set the school record for touchdown passes in a single game (six).

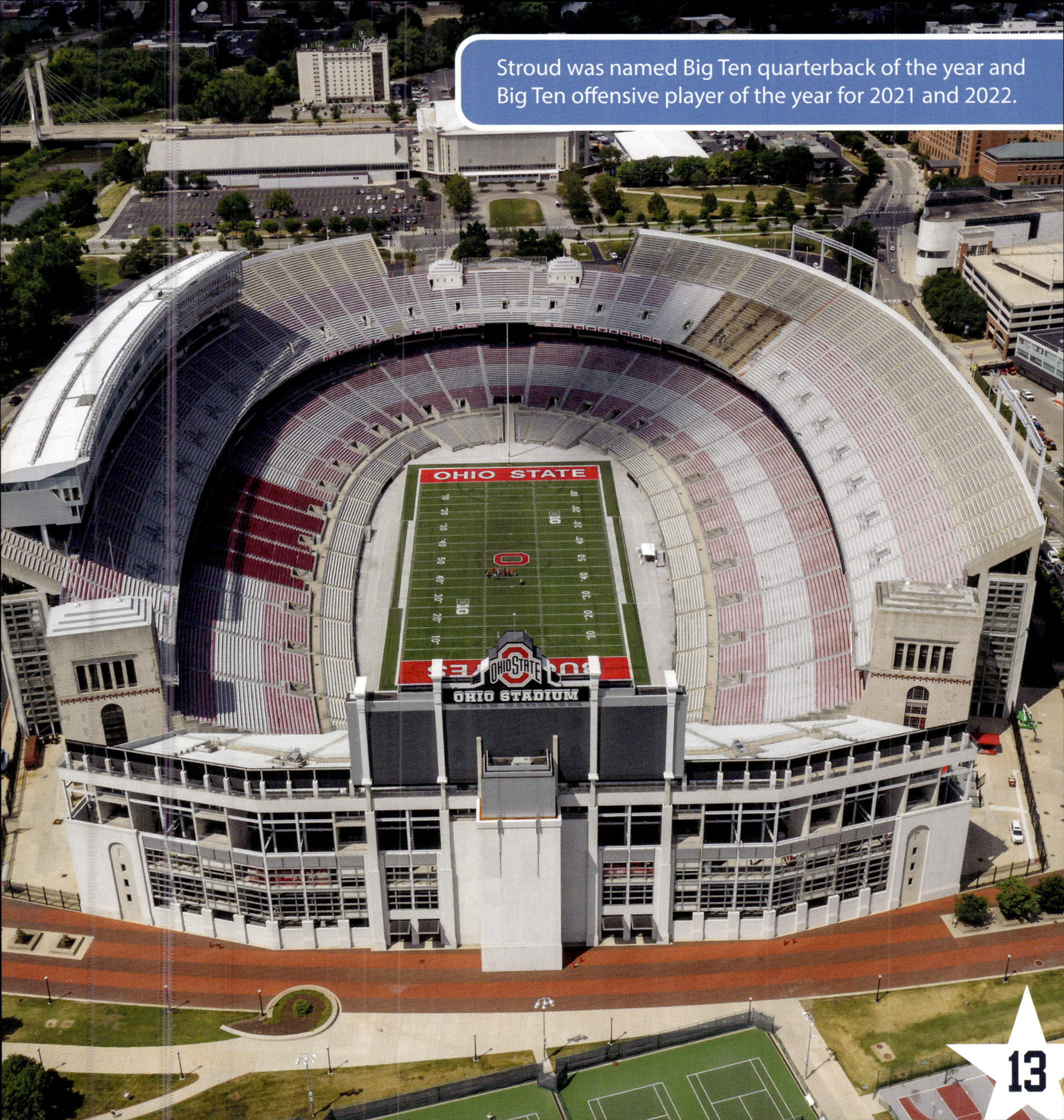

Stroud was named Big Ten quarterback of the year and Big Ten offensive player of the year for 2021 and 2022.

Stroud and the Buckeyes came close to reaching the Big Ten Football Championship Game, but they lost key games to the Michigan State Spartans. However, this didn't stop Stroud from **dominating** the Big Ten.

One of Stroud's greatest moments with the Buckeyes came in the 2022 **Rose Bowl**. Stroud led the team to a comeback win against the Utah Utes 48–45. During the game, Stroud threw for 573 yards (524 m) and 6 touchdowns. He broke records for OSU as well as the Rose Bowl!

WHAT THEY'RE SAYING

"C. J. has really grown in terms of his leadership this year . . . . He sees it almost as a coach right now. I know . . . he wants to win, and everything else is secondary."

—Ryan Day, Stroud's coach at OSU

During college, Stroud became the only two-time Heisman Trophy finalist in OSU history. This is a yearly award given to the most outstanding college football player.

THE 2023 NFL DRAFT

In January 2023, Stroud made a life-changing decision. He chose not to attend his remaining two years of college and to enter the 2023 NFL draft. This event, held once a year in April, gives NFL teams the chance to choose new players for their teams. It's a huge honor to get chosen in the first round of the draft.

Stroud was the second player taken in the draft. The Houston Texans chose him. This made him Ohio State's highest-drafted quarterback in history!

The only player taken higher than Stroud in 2023 was quarterback Bryce Young. Stroud and Young met while playing football in high school and continued to be friends through college.

THE HOUSTON TEXANS

The Houston Texans have been an NFL team since 2002. The Texans' first 10 years were not that great. However, they have won seven division championships since 2011. The Texans did not make it to the playoffs in 2023—but then they signed C. J. Stroud.

Stroud's first season with the Texans was a great success. Stroud became just the second rookie quarterback in the history of the NFL to win a playoff game. Stroud ended his first season with the AP Offensive Rookie of the Year award.

The Texans fell short during the 2024 playoffs, but they are excited about good things to come with C. J. Stroud.

WHAT'S NEXT?

Stroud is working to win football games for the Houston Texans. Many people think he's the next NFL GOAT.

In 2023, the Stroud family started the C. J. Stroud Foundation. Their first event was named "Quarterbacking Hunger." They gave out Thanksgiving food to 100 single mothers in Houston. Kimberly Stroud was very proud of her son. She said, "I'm really grateful [happy] that C. J. has taken the step . . . for a young voice in our **generation** to shed light on some of the issues that go on in this world."

WHAT THEY'RE SAYING

"In this league, everybody's looking for that quarterback . . . . It takes a special person to play that position and we're happy to have C. J. leading us."

—DeMeco Ryans, head coach of the Houston Texans

Whether he is dominating on the football field or giving back to the community, the road ahead for C. J. Stroud is looking very bright.

GLOSSARY

accurate: On target.

athlete: A person who is trained in or good at games and exercises that require physical skill, endurance, and strength.

championship: A contest to find out who is the best player or team in a sport.

conference: An association of sports teams.

dominate: To have a commanding position or controlling power over.

generation: All the people born and living at about the same time.

humble: Modest or meek in spirit or manner, rather than proud or bold.

offensive: Relating to the players in a sport who are attempting to score points.

resilient: Having the ability to recover from or adjust to misfortune or change.

Rose Bowl: An annual college championship game usually played on January 1 in Pasadena, California.

FOR MORE INFORMATION

BOOKS

Danks, Landon. *The Most Amazing NFL Stories Of All Time—For Kids!* Independently Published, 2023.

Hewson, Anthony K. *C. J. Stroud: Football Superstar.* Mendota Heights, MN: North Star Editions, 2024.

Mattern, Joanne. *The Houston Texans.* Minneapolis, MN: Bellwether Media, 2024.

WEBSITES

Official Site of the Houston Texans
www.houstontexans.com
Visit the home of the Texans to learn more about Stroud, the team's history, and much more.

Ohio State Buckeyes
ohiostatebuckeyes.com
Learn more about all of OSU's sports teams here.

Publisher's note to educators and parents: Our editors have carefully reviewed these websites to ensure that they are suitable for students. Many websites change frequently, however, and we cannot guarantee that a site's future contents will continue to meet our high standards of quality and educational value. Be advised that students should be closely supervised whenever they access the internet.

INDEX